Abingdon's
Easter Drama
COLLECTION 2

SHELBA SHELTON NIVENS

Abingdon Press

CONTENTS

JESUS IS COMING
(For Palm Sunday)

This is a dramatization of Jesus' triumphant entry into the city to begin a service of praise. Production is simple but a live donkey and co-operation of the entire congregation is needed.

PLAYING TIME: 10 minutes

PROPS: Donkey, large leaves, flowers, branches

CHARACTERS: **LEADERS**—*(This might be the pastor or music/worship leader)*
SINGERS AND PRAISERS—*(children, youth, adults) but several people should be prepared to lead.)*
JESUS
PHARISEES 1 AND 2
DONKEY CARETAKER—*(Someone responsible for handling donkey)*

COSTUMES: Biblical dress for Jesus. Dress for others optional.

LEADER: *(Stands in pulpit, reads from Mark 11:1-7)*
Near Jerusalem, Jesus said to two of his disciples, "Go to the village over there and you will find a colt upon which no man has ever sat. Loose him and bring him to me. If anyone says to you, 'Why do you do this?' tell him that the Lord has need of him and he will send the colt to me." So the disciples went into the village and found the colt tied, and they loose him. Some people standing there asked, "Why are you loosing the colt?" When they said to them what Jesus had commanded, the men let them go. So they brought the colt to Jesus and threw their cloaks across his back, and Jesus sat upon him.

(LEADER asks CONGREGATION to stand as for prayer. This will have the people on their feet, making it easier to get them outside. SINGERS begin praise song outside sanctuary.)

PRAISERS: *(Shout over sound of singing)*
Hosanna to the Son of David.

5

Blessed is he that cometh in the name of the Lord.
Hosanna in the highest.
Blessed be the kingdom of our father David.
Praises to the Lord.
Blessed be the king.
Praise him for his mighty works.
Praise his name forever.

(enter sanctuary) It's Jesus! Jesus is coming! *(to various individuals in congregation)*
Have you heard how he raised Lazarus from the dead?
He's performed many miracles.
He's coming this way.
Come with us to see him.
Hurry, he's getting nearer.
Can you hear the crowd singing his praises?
Hurry! Come with us!

(CONGREGATION moves outside. JESUS moves into view on donkey. SINGERS and PRAISERS move with him, spreading flowers, small branches. CONGREGATION joins singing.)

PHARISEE 1:   *(Waves hands, shouts)* Stop! Stop the singing. *(SINGERS, PRAISERS grow quieter.)* What are you people saying? Listen to yourselves. You shout as though he is your king.

PHARISEE 2:   You shout as though he is your lord. It is blasphemy. You must stop! *(SINGERS and PRAISERS begin loudly again.)*

PHARISEES: Stop! Stop this blasphemy at once. *(Singing and praising continue.)*

PHARISEE 1:   Jesus! Teacher! *(Singing, praising stop.)* Teacher, do you hear what the people are saying? You must rebuke them. Tell them to be quiet.

JESUS: Let them alone. The Lord must be praised. If the people cease to praise him, the stones would cry out in praise.

(SINGING and PRAISING begin again. JESUS moves to steps, dismounts, moves with CONGREGATION into sanctuary for service.)

KEEP PRAISING
(Palm Sunday Dramatization)

Production may be as elaborate or as simple as you choose. Few props are needed. Action moves from outside sanctuary up aisle to platform. Narrator on platform or behind scenes.

PROPS: Large leaves, flowers, small branches. Stools or benches. Swords or spears for soldiers. Money bag for Judas.

PLAYING TIME: 10 minutes

CHARACTERS: **NARRATORS 1 and 2** *(at each side of platform or behind scenes)*
MUSIC LEADER and **SINGERS** *(choir, children, or soloist)*
CROWD—includes disciples *(except Judas)*, other men, women, children.
PETER and **PERSONS** *(in Crowd)* **1, 2, 3, 4,** and **5** have brief lines.
OTHERS, including **CHILDREN**, ad lib.
JESUS
JUDAS
2 SOLDIERS
2 RELIGIOUS LEADERS
SPEAKER from audience

COSTUMES: Biblical dress.

NARRATOR 1: *(from John 11:43-48, 53, 55, 56)*
When Jesus raised Lazarus from the dead many Jewish leaders saw the miracle and finally believed on him. But some went away and told the Pharisees what Jesus had done.

Then the chief priests and Pharisees anxiously gathered together a council. "What are we to do?" they asked each other. "This man is doing many miracles. If we let him alone, everyone will start to believe on him, and the Romans will come and take away our positions and our government."

So, from that day forth they took counsel together to put him to death.

Now, the Jewish Passover celebration was drawing near. Many people from the country around Jerusalem went up to the city several days early to take part in the cleansing ceremony before the Passover began. They watched for Jesus at the Temple, asking among themselves, "What do you think? Will he come for the Passover feast?"

NARRATOR 2: (*from Mark 11:1, 7-10*)
Meanwhile, Jesus and his disciples were making their way toward Jerusalem. And as soon as the people heard that he was coming, they ran to meet him. Many of them spread their cloaks on the path before him. Others cut branches off the trees and spread these before him. And as they ushered him down the streets toward the temple, they shouted and sang his praises.

PERSON 1: (*over speaker, or loudly from outside main sanctuary door*)
Jesus is coming!

CROWD: (*loudly from outside sanctuary, claps, ad libs*)
Jesus is coming! God has given us a king! Make way for our king. Long live the King. Let all heaven rejoice. Glory to God in the highest heavens. Hosanna in the highest! Blessed is he that cometh in the name of the Lord! Blessed be the kingdom of our father David. Hail to the king of the universe.

(JESUS & CROWD enter sanctuary doors, move up center aisle. CROWD sings praise song, waves branches, spreads branches, flowers and coats before Jesus.)

(MUSIC LEADER asks CONGREGATION to stand and join in singing. JESUS takes seat on platform, stage center. CROWD gathers around him; some stand while others sit on floor, stools or front pews. After song, CONGREGATION is seated. SUGGESTED SONG: "Praise Him! Praise Him" or "Everybody Sing Praise to the Lord.")

NARRATOR 1: Not only men and women praised Jesus that day. But the children, too, shouted his praises, and sought to be near him.

CHILDREN: *(ad lib loudly)*
God bless Jesus. God bless the Son of David. Jesus is our king. Jesus is our friend. *(Move near Jesus.)*

(JESUS takes child on his knee, places arms around others. CHILDREN gather close to JESUS as they sing or during song by SOLOIST or CHOIR. Suggested SONG: "All Glory, Laud and Honor," or "Hosanna, Loud Hosanna." Or song may be omitted to shorten presentation.)

NARRATOR 2: People had come from everywhere for the Passover. There were merchants, farmers, housewives, teachers, students, loggers, builders. . . . ordinary people like you and me. And they all swapped stories about the things they had seen Jesus do. Many of them had experienced Jesus' touch on their own lives.

PERSON 1: Were you there on the mountainside the day He fed of 5,000 people with one small boy's lunch of fish and bread?

PERSON 2: I saw him raise Lazarus from the dead.

PERSON 3: I was blind from birth, but He touched my eyes and now I see.

PERSON 4: My sister had a blood disease for many years, but He healed her.

PERSON 5: I was once tormented by evil spirits, but He drove them all away.

Crowd: Praise God! Praise His name!

(SONG of praise and rejoicing—optional)

NARRATOR 1: The people had reason to rejoice that day. Here, at last, was the king who would rescue them from the iron fist of the Romans. Here was the Messiah, whom the prophets had been proclaiming down through the ages. It was a great day, indeed! As it is today when we have a great Sunday morning service—a great musical concert—or a series of great revival services. This first Palm Sunday was a time of great excitement, renewal, new commitments. The people *just knew* their lives would never be the same again.

NARRATOR 2: But Sunday ended. Monday morning came. Some of the people left and went back to their daily tasks. And forgot about Jesus.

(A few PERSONS from CROWD exit to seats in congregation, taking some of the CHILDREN with them.)

NARRATOR 1: However, the enthusiasm of others continued on into the next week. Crowds continued to gather in the temple to listen to Jesus' teachings.

(JESUS stands; CROWD shifts positions as they gather around him.)

NARRATOR 2: At one point Jesus cautioned the people:

JESUS: *(speaking to crowd and congregation from Matthew 14:7-13)* Nation will rise against nation and kingdom against kingdom. There will be famines, and pestilences, and earthquakes in many places. But all of these are only the beginning of the sorrows which will come. Some of you will be afflicted and killed, and hated by all nations for my name's sake. Many who believe on me now, will turn again to sin and come to hate and betray each other. False prophets will rise up to deceive many people. Because sin will abound in the world, the love of many will turn cold. But those who endure unto the end will be saved.

NARRATOR 2: The people vowed to stand true to Him—to continue worshiping him and telling others about Him.

CROWD: *(ad lib such as:)* No, we'll never go back on you. I'll always be true to you, Lord. Yes, we love you. I'll always praise you.

NARRATOR 2:   Peter voiced the sentiments of many of them.

PETER: *(stands, speaks loudly and boldly)* Why, Master, I would go to prison for you. I would even die for you.

NARRATOR 2:   Yes, the people loved him greatly. Or so they said. But before the week was out, their tune had drastically changed. Some drifted away. . . .

(A few more PERSONS from CROWD exit to pews. JESUS watches sadly.)

NARRATOR 2:   Others ran away frightened when signs of opposition came.

(Enter 2 SOLDIERS left. CROWD, except DISCIPLES, jump up and exit to pews. SOLDIERS stand waiting as JUDAS and 2 RELIGIOUS LEADERS enter right.)

NARRATOR 2:   Judas betrayed him. . . .

(JUDAS whispers with LEADERS and SOLDIERS. LEADER 1 hands him money bag. JUDAS leads them to JESUS, kisses his cheek, exits.)

NARRATOR 2:   Soldiers took him away to be crucified.

(SOLDIERS lead JESUS toward exit right. DISCIPLES run off left, except PETER who hesitantly follows JESUS.)

NARRATOR 2:   His disciples deserted him. And even Peter, who had vowed so earnestly that he would die for him, denied even knowing him.

SPEAKER FROM AUDIENCE: *(Stands, points to Peter)* That man is one of his followers. I saw him with Jesus.

PETER: No, I was not with him. I don't even know the man.

(Turns back following Jesus. Exits left, head down. JESUS, SOLDIERS, LEADERS exit right.)

NARRATOR 2:   And thus, less than a week, after his triumphant entry into the city where the people were singing his praises, Jesus was led alone—without one friend—to stand before the people who could condemn him to die.

(During above, SOLDIERS lead JESUS on to stand facing congregation. They all stand silently for few moments after reading ends, then exit right.)

NARRATOR 1:   *(from Luke 19:41-44)* A few days before his death, on the day He rode the donkey into Jerusalem, Jesus paused on a hill to look down upon the city. And in the midst of all the celebration and cheers, he wept. "You could have known the things which would bring you peace," he cried, "But now they are hid from your eyes. Now the day will come when your enemies will cast a trench about you and encircle you and hem you in on every side. They will lay you even with the ground, and your children within you. There will not be one stone left upon another because you refused to see the opportunity God offered you."

As we meet together on this Palm Sunday morning to commemorate the day of Jesus' triumphant entry into Jerusalem, might Jesus be looking down on us, too, and weeping? Is He looking ahead to this coming week to see the opposition and heartache that some of us will experience?

As we praise Him today, is he saying, "Oh, my child, how I want you to really understand what you are saying. How I want you to experience the real source of peace in your life."

We want to continue to praise Him this morning in this service. And may we all praise Him during the coming week as we go about our daily lives. Let's make a conscious effort this week to not be like the people who praised him on Sunday only to desert him before the week was out. May we not be as the people who got busy and forgot about him—or the religious leaders who condemned him because believing in him would mean a threat to their jobs or other positions in life. May we not be as Judas who valued monetary things more than God himself—the disciples who ran away because of fear—or Peter who denied even knowing him. Let's keep praising him in word, deed and attitude.

(MUSIC LEADER leads CONGREGATION in song of praise and dedication. Invitation might also be given here.)

SUPPER WITH JESUS

(A dramatization of Jesus' last supper with his disciples.)

PLAYING TIME: 30 minutes

SETTING: The Upper Room. A long table covered by a white cloth is stage center. 13 chairs are arranged around table as in suggested arrangement below. Small serving table is downstage right. Suggested seating and action will help prevent actors from blocking audience view of speakers.

SUGGESTED SEATING ARRANGEMENT:

	Thaddaeus	James 1	John	Jesus	Thomas	Matthew	
Philip							Judas
	James 2	Simon	Andrew	Bartholomew	Peter		

OTHER PROPS: Ceramic-type plates, bowls, glasses, pitchers. Large jar of purple drink. Basket, tray, bread, cheese, fruit.

CHARACTERS: Jesus and the 12 disciples

COSTUMES: Biblical dress

(PETER enters right carrying large basket filled with bread, cheese, fruit. Hums happily as he places items on tables and begins setting table for meal.)

(JOHN enters right, slowly, scowling. Carries large bowl, sets it on table, flops into chair.)

PETER: *(busily setting table)* Don't just sit, John! We have work to do. Jesus and the others will soon be here to eat the Passover meal.

JOHN: Then some of the others can help make preparations. This is not my kind of work, Peter. Why, at home I had servants to do this sort of thing for *me.*

PETER: But the master assigned this job to us, John. He entrusted you and me with the preparations. You know what that means, don't you?

JOHN: Yes. It means someone else is taking my place at Jesus' side, and listening to his teaching, while I am here doing drudgery.

PETER: No, no, John. You have the wrong attitude about it. As I see it, it means that Jesus trusts us—you and me—to get a job done. He is preparing us to be leaders in his kingdom. *(Moves closer with air of confidentiality)* Confidentially, I think you and I are the two disciples most important to Jesus.

JOHN: I have always felt that he loves me more than any of his other disciples. That's why I cannot understand why he sent me from his side to do—this. *(gestures with a wave of his hand over the table.)*

PETER: In case you haven't noticed, John, *you* are not doing— this. *(Imitates John's gesture.)* I am.

(Voices of other DISCIPLES are heard offstage right.)

PETER: *(works hurriedly)* I hear them downstairs now.

JOHN: *(jumps up and begins helping set table.)*

(JESUS and other DISCIPLES enter left, move toward table. DISCIPLES, except JUDAS, talk excitedly among selves about things they have seen Jesus do

and things they have heard him say. NOTE: Participants need to be familiar with the words and works of Jesus as recorded in the Gospels in order to ad lib here.)

(PETER continues to move from table to table, preparing for the meal. ANDREW goes to help him. JOHN hurries to seat JESUS. THOMAS takes chair at Jesus' left. JOHN tilts chair at Jesus' right against table to reserve for himself, then starts pouring wine into the glasses. JAMES 1 lowers the chair and sits down.)

JOHN: James, you know that is my place beside Jesus. You can just find another for yourself.

(JAMES 1 moves to another place.)

PHILIP: John, you should be happy that your brother desires to be near our Lord.

JOHN: But that is my place. I always sit beside Jesus. *(Finishes pouring, places pitcher near Jesus' plate, sits.)*

THADDAEUS: James, why do you allow John to push you around?

JAMES 1: *(shrugs)* Oh, because it is easier to give in to him, I suppose.

(DISCIPLES continue to talk quietly among selves. JESUS stands to get their attention.)

PETER: *(at serving table)* Quiet, everyone! The Master has something to say to us.

(Immediate quiet. All eyes on Jesus.)

JESUS: With deep longing I have looked forward to this hour. I am anxious to eat this Passover meal with you before my suffering begins. And I must tell you now that I will not eat it again until what it represents has occurred in the kingdom of God.

JAMES 1: *(to Thaddaeus)* Suffering? He speaks as though it's about to happen.

15

THADDAEUS:	He told us when we were on our way to Jerusalem that he would soon be condemned to death and be mocked and scourged.
PHILIP:	*(jumping to feet)* No! It cannot be! Such horrors will not befall our master.
JAMES 1:	Be still, Simon. Don't you recall how our Lord rebuked Peter for saying those very words? He said that his death is God's will.
PETER:	Let the Master speak.
JESUS:	*(Looking around table)* You call me Master and Lord, and you are right to do this. It is true. And if I am your Master and Lord, you ought to obey the things I have taught you. I know all of you well, and I know that you all do not obey. And one of you is about to betray me.

(DISCIPLES look around at each other murmuring.)

JESUS:	You have read in the Scriptures, "One who eats supper with me will betray me." This will soon come to pass. I am reminding you of it now so that when it happens you will know that I am He of whom the Scriptures speak. *(sits.)*
ANDREW:	Bartholomew, do you recall the scripture?
BARTHOLOMEW:	The Psalmist wrote, "Mine own familiar friend which did eat of my bread, hath lifted up his heel against me."
THADDAEUS:	He spoke also of false witnesses rising up.
BARTHOLOMEW:	And the prophet Isaiah said the Promised One would be oppressed and afflicted and brought as a lamb to the slaughter.

(Silence. DISCIPLES turn to look at JESUS. PETER and ANDREW move quietly to places at table. SOFT MUSIC begins.)

JESUS:	*(Picks up bread and stands. Lifts face heavenward to pray.)*

16

Our Father, we thank you for all your provisions. Thank you for the bread we are about to break together. *(To disciples as He begins to break bread, and as SOFT MUSIC begins)* This is my body given for you. Eat it in remembrance of me. *(Passes out bread.)*

(JUDAS hesitates before taking bread. Holds it, looking at it quietly as others eat reverently.)

JESUS: *(pours wine into glass, lifts it, looks heavenward.)* Thank you, Father, for this, the fruit of the vine. *(To disciples)* Pass this among yourselves and each of you drink, for it is my blood of the new testament, which is shed for the remission of your sins. *(Refills glass when emptied, or a separate glass may be used for each person.)*

(DISCIPLES pass wine. JUDAS hesitates about taking it.)

PETER: Judas! The glass!

(JUDAS takes glass, lifts hesitantly, barely sips. Other DISCIPLES drink reverently. Then there is silence as JESUS sits down and they begin to pass food, serve plates and eat. They might break off pieces of bread and dip into bowls, eat cheese with fingers, etc.)

(ANDREW stands, moves with serving bowl or tray toward serving table, pausing to whisper briefly to PETER. PETER picks up pitcher, stands, follows him to serving table.)

ANDREW: Peter, do you know who will betray Jesus? Has he told you?

PETER: No, but I have my suspicions. I know it is not me. I could never do such a thing to our Lord.

(MATTHEW moves to serving table. THOMAS and BARTHOLOMEW whisper to each other, stand and follow him.)

MATTHEW: Peter, I know you are important to Jesus. Has he told you who will betray him?

THOMAS: *He* is important? Why do you say Peter is so important? Surely he is no more important to the Master than I.

BARTHOLOMEW: I am the one who is most familiar with the prophesies. If Jesus were to tell someone it would surely be me.

JAMES 1: Master, tell us who will betray you.

(JUDAS drops head.)

OTHER DISCIPLES: Yes, tell us. Who will it be?

JESUS: *(stands, points, letting finger and his eyes move slowly over all the DISCIPLES and the audience as he speaks.)* It is one of you. One of you who eats at the table with me—one of you in this room tonight—will betray me. I must die as part of God's plan. But as for the one who will betray me—it would be better for him if he had never been born. *(His eyes come back to rest on JUDAS.)*

(JUDAS drops his head. Other DISCIPLES look questioningly at each other. Several put hand to breast as though silently asking, "Is it I?")

DISCIPLES: *(except JUDAS):* Is it I? Is it I, Master?

(JESUS shakes head, indicating "no," at each. DISCIPLES at serving table huddle to whisper. Other DISCIPLES, except JUDAS, lean over table, whispering to each other.)

JUDAS: Rabbi, is it I?

(JESUS stars as JUDAS silently for a moment, then nods in the affirmative. JUDAS drops head to hands. JESUS sits, drops head.)

JOHN: *(loudly)* I am certainly not the one. I love him too much! *(Turns to throw arms around Jesus with face against his shoulder. OTHERS continue to talk among themselves.)*

ANDREW: Peter, why don't you tell John to ask him.

PETER: *(calls quietly)* John.

(JOHN looks up. PETER motions for him to come over to him. JOHN joins DISCIPLES at serving table.)

PETER: John, you are seated close to the Master. Ask him who it is that would do this terrible thing.

(JOHN nods, returns to stand beside JESUS. OTHERS at table continue whispering.)

JOHN: Lord, tell me—who will betray you?

JESUS: It is the one to whom I will give a sop after I have dipped it.

DISCIPLES at serving table: *(to each other)* Did you hear? What did he say? Did he say the name?

(JESUS dips bread in bowl and gives to JUDAS. JOHN places hand over mouth in surprise. JUDAS takes bread, drops eyes.)

JESUS: Go, Judas. Hurry. Do what you must do now.

THOMAS: Where is he sending Judas?

BARTHOLOMEW: He carries the money bag. Perhaps he is going to pay for our food tonight.

PETER: No, John and I took care of that.

(JUDAS clutches money bag. Pulls robe about him, avoiding eyes of others as he slips out the door.)

JESUS: *(stands, looks around at Disciples)* There is something I must tell you now.

(DISCIPLES gather around to hear. PETER stands behind chair vacated by Judas. NOTE: Be sure no one blocks audience view of Jesus.)

JESUS: I have such a short time before I must go away and leave you. So I am giving a new commandment to you now. *(Pauses to look pointedly at Disciples and audience.)* You must love each other as much as I love you. When the world sees the way you love each other, they will know that you are my disciples.

PETER: Master, where are you going?

JESUS:	Where I am going, you cannot go now. But you will follow me later.
PETER:	But why can't I go with you now? I am ready to go anywhere for you, Lord. I would even die for you.

(Other DISCIPLES agree)

JESUS:	*(looks at them sadly, shakes head.)* No, you are not ready to die for me. This very night you will all forsake me. *(DISCIPLES murmur denial)* And you, Peter, before the cock crows tomorrow morning, will deny that you even know me. Not once, Peter, but three times you will deny me.
PETER:	No! Not I! I . . .
JESUS:	*(holds up a hand to quiet PETER.)* Peter, Satan is determined to have you. He wants to sift you like wheat. But I have been praying for you that your faith will not completely fail. So after you have repented and turned back to me, I ask that you strengthen and build up the faith of your brothers. *(To Disciples and audience.)* Do not let all of this trouble you. You trust in God, so trust in me. In my father's house are many mansions. I'm just going on ahead to prepare them for your coming. Then I will return for you so you may always be where I am. You already know where I am going. And you know how to get there.
THOMAS:	Lord, we don't know. We have no idea where you are going. How can we know the way?
JESUS:	I am the Way, Thomas. And the Truth and the Life. No one can get to the Father except through me. If you know me, you know the Father. When you see me, you see the Father.
PHILIP:	Master, show us the Father himself, then we will be satisfied.
JESUS:	Oh, Philip. Don't you even yet know who I am? Do

you still not understand even after all the time I have been with you? Don't you believe me when I say that I am in the Father and the Father is in me? Simply trust what I say. Or at least believe because of all the miracles you have seen me do.

(DISCIPLES agree that his miracles are proof.)

JESUS: *(to everyone)* And another thing—it is up to you in this room to be my witnesses to the world. Since you have been with me from the beginning and know me, you must tell everyone about me.

(DISCIPLES nod, ad lib commitment.)

JESUS: I am not going away and leave you comfortless. For when I leave, the Holy Spirit will come to be with you and will later live within you. He will remind you of all that I have said and help you to understand it. And through the Holy Spirit, I will live within you and will reveal myself to you. But let me caution you—worldly people cannot understand or receive the Holy Spirit, for they are not looking for Him and do not recognize him.

PHILIP: But, Lord, why do you reveal yourself only to your disciples?

JESUS: Because only those who love me and obey me can really know me. And remember, you don't really love me if you do not obey me. If you love me, you will do what I tell you to do.

DISCIPLES: We do love you. We will obey you.

JESUS: Then, let me stress to you that if you love me, you will also love each other. As a matter of fact, I command you to love each other as much as I love you. *(Pauses to look pointedly around at members of congregation.)* And, oh, how I love you! I love you as much as the Father loves me. I love you so much that I give my life for you. *(to Disciples)* Even now, the evil one approaches to take me. He has no real power over me, but I willingly do what the Father's plan requires because I love the Father—and you. So, love one another.

(DISCIPLES place arms around each other's shoulders, turn to assure each other and Jesus of their love.)

JESUS: Remember this—you can have no greater love than to lay down your own life for a friend. Give up your own desires for those of your brother. There must be no more bickering between you about who is more important—about doing my work—about hurt feelings or slights. There is enough hate and contention in the world. There is to be none among those who say they love me. Obey me and you will find true happiness.

There is so much more I want to tell you, but you are not able to understand it now. Some day, you *will* understand—when you have received the Holy Spirit. But now what I want you to understand is that I have all the glory of the Father, and in just a little while I will be gone to the Father.

DISCIPLES: *(to each other)* What does he mean? What is he talking about? Gone to the father? I don't understand.

JESUS: I know you are wondering what I mean. But listen closely when I tell you this—there will be rejoicing in the world over what is going to happen to me, and you will weep. But you will see me again and your tears will turn to joy. You will be able to go directly to the Father in my name and your prayers will be answered. The Father loves you because you love me. Yes, I came into the world from the father, and soon I will leave the world and return to the father.

PHILIP: At last you are speaking where we can understand you, Lord! And it is plain that you know everything. I believe that you came from God.

(DISCIPLES agree)

JESUS: Oh, Father, the world does not know you. But, these that believe in me know that you sent me. I will continue to reveal you to them so that your love may live within them, and I in them. Amen.

(Song of consecration and invitation might be used here.)

AS THE CROWDS CHEER HIM
(Portrayal of Mary, the Mother of Jesus)

This is a monologue by Mary as she listens and watches Jesus and the cheering crowd approach from a distance and pass on by. No visible props are needed, but taped sound of the cheering crowd will help to make the reading more effective. Mary should be in biblical dress.

PLAYING TIME: 10 minutes

SOUND EFFECTS: taped sounds of the crowd as they cheer Jesus and shout, "Hail to our king. Hosanna! Blessed is the king that comes in the name of the Lord," etc.

(Enter MARY left, moving down center with head lowered, lost in thought. Suddenly, distant shouts and cheers of the crowd are heard. MARY lifts head quickly, alert to the sound. Sound may be lowered as she speaks.)

MARY: Listen! Do you hear the shouting? They're crying, "Hosanna! Blessed is the king that comes in the name of the Lord." *(Points toward imaginary spot in the distance to her right, between stage and audience)* And, look! Can you see him there? It's Jesus! Yes, the carpenter from Nazareth. Jesus, my son.

(Peering into the distance, watching the procession) Great crowds of people have come out to meet him—and to cheer him. He's riding upon a donkey—just a lowly donkey—but they salute him as though he really is a king. They're spreading their cloaks and branches of the palm tree before him. They're waving the palms, and they keep shouting. Do you hear what they're saying? "Blessed is the King sent from the Lord!"

But I wonder if they understand their own words. How many of them really feel the words they speak? How many are only letting themselves be carried along on waves of excitement that shall soon pass? Do any of them understand that he really is their king sent from God? But, then, I'm not sure that I, his own mother, understand it myself.

It seems so long ago that the angel came to me—telling me that I would bear the child of the Most High God. So long ago that it seems almost a dream. So long ago that I had almost put the angel's words from my mind—until recent days. Things I've seen Jesus do lately—things I've heard him say—have caused me to remember—although, sometimes, I'd rather not.

Of course, I think his miracles are wonderful. Any mother would be proud. And I can't help but feel a touch of pride as I listen to the people shout his praises. Hear them? They're drawing closer. Can you hear what they're saying?

(SOUND of crowd grows loud again, then diminishes as MARY speaks.)

"Blessed be the name of Jesus!" they cry. "Hosanna in the highest!"

But what does all of this really mean? Where will it go from here? Many of these people who cheer him have seen his miracles, too. No doubt many of them were there in the crowd when he fed the five thousand. Some of them owe their sight—their very lives to him. It has been spread abroad that he raised Lazarus from the dead. And now they expect him to do even more great and mighty things for them.

I can't help wondering, though, what *they* are willing to do for *him*. They shout his praises now. Will they remember this day and stand true to him if trouble comes?

And I have a feeling that it is to come. Even now, as he sits up on the donkey listening to the cheers of the crowd, there seems to be an air of sadness about him. See? *(Indicates with hand that he is passing before the audience)* It is there in his eyes. They reflect such— sadness. What is it he sees out there ahead of him? What can he see beyond the shouts, the waving palms and smiling faces? Oh, I wish I knew. Or, perhaps, I'm better off not knowing.

Perhaps it is only a mother's heart that causes me to fear this way. But I keep recalling bits and pieces of things I've heard him say about the Heavenly Father's plan to redeem his people: "Without shedding of blood there is no remission of sins," he told me one day. "And it is not possible that the blood of bulls and of goats should take away sins."

Why was I afraid to ask him to explain his words to me? Why should these words frighten me so? What do they have to do with my son? My son who even now rides through the crowd being proclaimed as their king? *(Indicates with hand that crowd is passing on by.)*

Suddenly, I seem to hear again the voice of John the day he baptized Jesus. "Behold, the lamb of God," he said. "He shall take away the sins of the world."

The sins of the world . . . ? Oh! *(Hand to heart)* Oh, No! *(Eyes heavenward)* Father, please! Tell me it's not so! Not, Jesus. *(Indicates with hand and eyes that Jesus and Crowd have passed on by.)* Not my son!

(Drops head, sinks to floor.)

(Curtain, light out, or music)

AT THE CRUCIFIXION

(Portrayal of Mary, the Mother of Jesus)

In this monologue Mary watches the crucifixion while recalling Jesus as a child. It might be used for a special Maundy Thursday or Good Friday service. No props are needed. Taped sound effects are optional. You might choose to use some or all of those suggested, or Mary's speech and actions only might suggest what she is seeing and hearing. Mary should be in biblical dress.

PLAYING TIME: 6 minutes

SOUND EFFECTS: General crowd noises, coarse laughter, jeering voices, women wailing, nails being driven into wood, voice of Jesus.

(Sound of jeering voices: "I hope that cross is good and strong. He may have to hang there a long time." "Yeah! It may take awhile for such a great king to die!" "Some king! Just look at him now!" Coarse laughter.)

(Enter MARY left, moving quickly down center with hands clasped to her breast. Stops, stares at a point offstage right as though watching as Jesus moves up Golgotha Hill.)

MARY: Oh, Father! How can a mother's heart bear such agony?

Oh, my son! To see you treated so cruelly! That heavy cross on your shoulders! *(Shakes head sadly)* He was already so weak from all the scourgings and the all-night mockery.

(Gasps, hands to head) Oh! He's falling beneath the load. Father, please help him. . . .

There! Someone does care. Someone—a large, dark man?—has stepped forward to help. He's taking the cross on his own shoulders. He carrying it up the hill for Jesus.

But, he is still so weak. . . . And the blood still trickles from cuts made by the lash of the whip. And that horrible crown of thorns! Oh! There's blood where the thorns have pierced his brow.

26

How many times I kissed that smooth young brow while he lay sleeping in his bed. How many times I cooled it with damp cloths to help ease the discomfort of childhood illness. So vividly now, I see the angel as he appeared to me that night telling me that I would bear a child. "Mary, thou art blessed among women," said the angel.

And I *was* blessed. I truly was. He was such a perfect baby. *(Smiles in remembrance.)* So tiny! So precious.

Oh, he cried—like all babies cry. And there were times—most of the time while he was growing up— when the angel's visit really did seem only a dream. For he was such a typical little boy. He could get so dirty! He loved playing with Joseph's carpenter's tools, and would come in with his little hands all bruised and cut and bleeding. . . .

(Sound of hammer slowly driving nail and the voices of women wailing. MARY jerks, turns attention back to the cross, hand to heart.) Oh! Father! They're putting nails through those hands. The hands that reached out to heal them when they were sick, to feed them when they were hungry, to lift them up out of the misery of their sins. The hands that reached out to them with so much love.

(Sound of hammer.)

Oh! How can they when he loved them so?

It seemed he just could never do enough for these people. And they demanded so much. He would push and push himself to reach more and more of them. He went for days without food and sleep, never thinking of himself. Only of others. Oh, how he loved them! And now, they are crucifying him! How can they be so cruel? How can they forget so soon?

Even now, as his life's blood streams from his body, he looks down on them with love and compassion. . . .

And, what is that he's saying? *(Pauses to listen.)* Father, forgive them? Forgive them?! While blood trickles into his eyes and gushes from that horrible hole in his side?

Oh, their terrible laughter! And what is it they shout? *(Listens)* You saved others, now save yourself? Come down from the cross? If only he *could* come down. . . .

But, no. . . . No! No! He's gone. *(Face to hands briefly, then looks back at "cross," and quickly turns away again.)* No! I cannot bear to see his broken body hanging there. Oh, Jesus, Jesus, Jesus. Jesus, my son Jesus, is gone. *(Drops head.)*

(Lights suddenly dim.)

(Head jerks up) What . . . ? What's happening? *(Looks around in fear.)* Why is it becoming so dark? *(Looks heavenward)* Father?! Father?! Have you hidden your face, too? Can you not bear to look upon such a cruel world? Does the Almighty God hide his face at such a terrible act of rejection. . . ?

(Complete darkness. Sound of rolling thunder.)

AFTER THE RESURRECTION

(Portrayal of Mary, the Mother of Jesus)

This monologue by Mary is designed for use on Easter Sunday morning. No props or sound effects are needed. Mary should be in biblical dress.

PLAYING TIME: 3 minutes

MARY: What is that you say? He's no longer in the tomb? Jesus, my son, is alive? He *is* resurrected? Then, it must all be true!

And now, so many things are clear to me.

"I must be about my father's business," he told me when he was only twelve years old. And later he told temple leaders "Destroy this temple, and in three days, I will raise it up."

(Thoughtfully) Now I see what he meant. *This* is the third day. The temple is himself. He did not bring himself down from the cross—although he could have done so—because that, too, was his Father's business. It was a part of the plan. God, the Father's great plan to redeem his people. The plan for Jesus to bear the sins of the world to a cruel cross. The plan for Jesus to die in their stead.

They did tear down the temple—those evil men. But, now he is raised again. In power and in glory, he is raised! And he can never be destroyed again.

Jesus is alive! My son, Jesus!

My son? Yes. He was my son. But he is, oh, so much more! He is Jesus my Lord. He is Jesus the Savior of the world. God made manifest in flesh to dwell for awhile among us. And now he lives again.

Oh, thank you, my Father. Thank you, thank you, thank you. Jesus lives! He lives now and forever more!

29

ALL THIS POWER

PLAYING TIME: 15 minutes

PROPS: Basket for Mary Magdalene. Blanket rolled and tied, wrapped in white sheet to represent body of Jesus. Large cave-like "tomb" and "rock" to roll away from its mouth.

SOUND EFFECTS: Taped sound for thunder or earthquake. Hammer driving nails into wood. Voice of Jesus, Voices 1, 2, and 3, other jeering voices and laughter in the crowd at the cross.

CHARACTERS: **NARRATOR**
3 OR 4 MEN to carry "body" of Jesus
3 OR 4 WOMEN to mourn
GUARDS 1 AND 2
MARY MAGDALENE
ANGEL
JESUS

COSTUMES: Long white robe with full sleeves for Angel. Long white, flowing, hooded robe for Jesus.

SCENE: Tomb stage right. Jesus is concealed inside tomb before service begins.

NARRATOR: *(Begins reading as part of regular worship service from Matthew 27:27-31 KJV)* Then the soldiers of the governor took Jesus into the common hall, and gathered unto him the whole band of soldiers. And they stripped him, and put on him a scarlet robe. And when they had plaited a crown of thorns, they put it upon his head, and a reed in his right hand: and they bowed the knee before him, and mocked him, saying, Hail, King of the Jews! And they spit upon him, and took the reed, and smote him on the head. And after that they had mocked him, they took the robe off of him, and put his own raiment on him, and led him away to crucify him.

(SOUND of hammer driving nails. Then, voices over.)

VOICE 1:   Hey, King of the Jews. You saved others. Now, let us see you save yourself. *(Jeering laughter and calls.)*

VOICE 2:   Yeah. You, who can destroy the temple and build it back in three days, show us how you can save yourself . . .

VOICE3:   You claimed to have so much trust in God. Let him deliver you now—if he will have you. *(Laughter, jeers)*

VOICE OF JESUS: Father, forgive them for they know not what they do.

VOICE 1:   Father forgive them? He calls God father? Hey! If you're really the son of God, come down from that cross.

VOICE 2:   Come on down, and then maybe we'll believe in you. Show us all this power you claim to have.

(SOUND of thunder/earthquake)

(SILENCE)

VOICE OF JESUS: Father, into thy hands I commit my spirit.

(SOUND of thunder. LIGHTS flash, go out. SILENCE.)

(LIGHTS on low)

MEN enter up aisle carrying sheet-wrapped "body." WOMEN follow at a distance, crying softly, watch as MEN place body in tomb, roll "stone" over the door, kneel and bow head briefly. Exit MEN. Exit WOMEN.)

NARRATOR: *(Matthew 27:62-66 KJV)* Now the next day, that followed the day of the preparation, the chief priests and Pharisees came together unto Pilate, Saying, Sir, we remember that that deceiver said, while he was yet alive. After three days I will rise again. Command therefore that the sepulcher be made sure until the third day, lest his disciples come by night, and steal him away, and say unto the people, He is risen from the dead: so the last error shall be worse than the first. Pilate said unto them, Ye have a watch: go your way, make it as sure as ye can. So they went, and made the sepulcher sure, sealing the stone, and setting a watch.

(GUARDS 1 and 2 enter and "seal" tomb door. Guard 1 takes station stage left to stand guard, Guard 2 stage right. Stand for few moments straight and alert, eyes ahead.)

GUARD 1: *(to Guard 2)* I cannot understand why we must stand guard over a dead man.

GUARD 2: While he was yet living, he said he would rise again in three days.

GUARD 1: Rise, ha! He's as dead as any corpse I ever saw.

GUARD 2: *(Moves stage left to GUARD 1)* The Jewish leaders fear that his followers will steal his body and say he is alive. To tell you the truth, I think they also fear his power over the people.

GUARD 1: Power? How much power can a dead man have?

(SOUND of thunder/earthquake. LIGHTS flash. GUARDS fall to floor, hide faces. ANGEL enters to tomb, moves stone aside. Steps back few paces, extending arms upward. As JESUS steps from tomb, his hooded robe, flashing lights, Angel and flowing sleeves of Angel robe partially conceal him from audience. Exit JESUS and ANGEL behind tomb. LIGHTS out. SILENCE.)

(LIGHTS on. GUARDS still huddle on floor stage left as MARY MAGDALENE enters up aisle, crying, carrying basket.)

MARY MAGDALENE: *(to tomb.)* The stone! It's been rolled away. *(Runs to opening in tomb, bends, looks inside.)* He is gone! They have taken away my lord! Where have they put him?! *(Stands crying, face in hands.)*

JESUS: *(enters)* Woman? Why are you crying? Whom are you seeking?

MARY MAGDALENE: *(lifts face)* Oh! Sir, are you the gardener? Can you help me? The body of my Lord is gone. If you moved him from here, please tell me where you have lain him and I will take him away. *(Cries into hands.)*

JESUS: Mary?

MARY MAGDALENE: *(Startled, looks up)* Master?! Master, is it really you? You are alive?! Oh . . . ! *(Reaches out to him.)*

JESUS: No. Do not touch me. I am not yet ascended to my Father. I want you to go to my brethren and tell them that I ascend to my Father and your Father, and to my God and your God. Say that I want them to go to Galilee where I will meet them.

MARY MAGDALENE: Oh, yes, my Lord. I will go. I will do as you say. *(Starts off hurriedly.)*

(Exit JESUS)

(MARY MAGDALENE stops, looks back, hurries down aisle to exit as GUARDS rise from floor.)

GUARD 1: Wow! Did you see that? Man, that's power!

GUARD 2: Let's get out of here. *(Moves quickly toward exit.)*

GUARD 1: *(Goes to peer in tomb. Raises up, shakes head.)* That's some power! *(exits, shaking head in awe.)*

NARRATOR: Yes, that is *some* power. The power of our resurrected Lord. And this power is available to you and me. Later on the day of his resurrection, and at various times during the next several days, Jesus appeared to his followers. "Peace be unto you," he told them. "As my Father hath sent me, even so send I you." And "Go ye into all the world and preach the gospel to every creature. He that believeth and is baptized shall be saved, but he that believeth shall not be damned." And He gave to those believers—and to us—the power of his own Holy Spirit. The power to help and minister to others. The power to overcome difficulties in our own lives. Power over grief, depression, discouragement, illness, death, sin and the grave.

(Appropriate song. You might use invitation here.)

PASS IT ON

This is a dramatization of the women at the empty tomb, to begin a service of joy and celebration on Easter Sunday. It is designed for easy production. Few props are needed.

PLAYING TIME: 10 minutes

PROPS AND SCENERY: Baskets and jars for woman. Tomb is painted on free-standing screen. Potted plants to represent garden.

CHARACTERS: **MARY MAGDALENE**—woman Jesus healed of seven demons
OTHER MARY—sister of Jesus' mother Mary, wife of Alphaeus
SALOME—wife of Zebedee, mother of disciples James and John
ANGEL
CHOIR

COSTUMES: White robe for Angel. Biblical dress for women.

(TOMB is downstage left. Enter right MARY MAGDALENE, OTHER MARY, SALOME with baskets and jars of spices and ointments.)

OTHER MARY: How can the day dawn so beautiful and bright as this when there is so much darkness within our souls?

MARY MAGDALENE: I feel as though my world ended with Jesus.

SALOME: He brought such hope into our lives. Everyone said he was to be our Savior, or Deliverer. Why, I, myself, had hopes of my own two sons, James and John, sitting one on his left and the other on his right when he came into his kingdom. But, now He is dead. All hope is gone.

MARY MAGDALENE: I feel that I just cannot bear it. It was he who gave me my life again. Demons had destroyed me. I was tortured day and night. I wanted only to die. And then I heard about this man called Jesus. . . . *(breaks down crying.)*

34

OTHER MARY: *(places arm around Mary Magdalene)* We all are sorely grieved over what has happened. He was my own dear sister Mary's son, you know. How it hurts me to look upon her sadness. She was standing right there near the cross, witnessing his agony, when he died. *(Cries into her shawl.)*

SALOME: But we must not stand here weeping. This is the dawn of the third day. The law of the Sabbath has already prevented a proper burial. We must prepare his body right away. *(Looks in basket)* Mary, did you bring the special ointment we prepared?

MARY MAGDALENE: *(Drying eyes)* I have it. But here—you take it, Salome. *(Gives bottle to SALOME)* I don't think I can bear to look upon his poor, lifeless form again.

SALOME: *(briskly)* Of course you can. Did we not all minister to him in life? Thus, this one last thing we shall all do together for him, also.

MARY MAGDALENE: You are right. I must do this for him. But hurry so we may finish this sad work as quickly as possible. *(Looks around)* I was certain it was near this spot that they laid him.

SALOME: He was laid in the new tomb over there. *(indicates direction)* My eyes were dimmed by tears, but I made special note of the spot so I could return with spices.

(MARY MAGDALENE moves sadly to tomb.)

OTHER MARY: But, Salome, a heavy stone was rolled over the opening. I heard that the soldiers sealed it in place. How shall we roll it away?

SALOME: Perhaps we should have asked one of the men to . . .

MARY MAGDALENE: *(from tomb)* Mary! Salome! Come quickly! The stone has been rolled away.

OTHER MARY, SALOME: *(look at each other in surprise.)* But . . . Who could have done it? What does it mean?

MARY MAGDALENE: *(bends to look inside tomb)* Oh, No-o-o-o! He is not here! He is gone!

SALOME: Gone? He can't be! *(Hurries to look inside tomb.)*

OTHER MARY: *(Hurries to look inside tomb.)* It is true. He is gone!

(WOMEN stare at each other in surprise, start to cry.)

ANGEL: *(enters from behind tomb)* Why are you crying?

MARY MAGDALENE: *(Wails)* Because they have taken away the body of my Lord—and I don't know where they have laid him.

OTHER MARY: It is an angel of the Lord!

(WOMEN fall to knees.)

ANGEL: Do not be afraid. Get up. Are you looking for Jesus, the Nazarene who was crucified?

(WOMEN rise)

MARY MAGDALENE: Yes. But we cannot find him.

ANGEL: Why are you so surprised? Did he not tell you that the Messiah would be betrayed into the power of evil men and be crucified? And that he would rise again after three days?

OTHER MARY: *(Nodding slowly.)* Yes. He did tell us that.

SALOME: It was back in Galilee . . .

MARY MAGDALENE: I remember . . .

ANGEL: Then why are you here looking in a tomb for someone who is alive? Jesus is not here. He has come back to life.

OTHER MARY: *(in awe)* My sister's son is alive? He is actually the Messiah?

SALOME: (*in awe*) Jesus? The Messiah? The Deliverer?

MARY MAGDALENE: (*Joyfully*) Yes! Oh, yes! It is true! I know it is true.
                 Jesus is the Messiah! The Savior! My Lord! And he is
                 alive!

OTHER MARY, SALOME: Jesus has risen! He lives!

ANGEL: Then go and tell his disciples. He will meet you in
                 Galilee just as he told you before he died.

SALOME: Yes! We must tell the others. I must tell my sons.

OTHER MARY: I must tell his mother, my sister.

MARY MAGDALENE: We must tell everyone. Jesus lives!

*(WOMEN hurry joyfully down aisle, exclaiming loudly to people in audience
right and left)*
                 Jesus is alive
                 He lives!
                 Pass it on!
                 Tell your neighbor!
                 Tell everyone!
                 He's the Messiah!
                 He's the Savior!
                 He is Lord!
                 He lives!
                 He lives forever!
                 etc. etc.

CHOIR: (*Joyful music such as "He Lives." CHOIR LEADER might
                 ask congregation to sing also.*)

THE HOLY LAMB

This presentation moves from prophecies concerning the coming of Jesus as the Lamb of God, through His birth and death to His resurrection. Songs and reading of prophecies over parts of the action help to shorten playing time. You may shorten it more by omitting some of the songs. Although production calls for a number of characters, plus the choir, most have small speaking parts, no lines at all, or only ad lib as part of a group. Some actors may play more than one roll.

Scene changes can be very simple, as suggested here, but if space permits, you might use more elaborate sets on a variety of levels or in different areas of auditorium. Additional scenery flats or moving scenery might also be used.

PLAYING TIME: 45 minutes

PROPS AND SCENERY: Stool for Mary. Manger and doll. Live lamb if possible; if not, a toy one. Cross. Hammer. Scenery flat with trees painted on it to place in front of cross. Tomb and rock for the door.

SOUND EFFECTS: Hammer driving nails. Sound of thunder. Mob noises with voices saying things such as: "He says he is God. He ought to die. He blasphemes the true God. He stirs up trouble everywhere he goes." NOTE: Mob noises can be accomplished with only a few voices and two tape recorders. Make the first tape then play it while recording it and the voices a second time, then a third time, etc. until desired effect.

CHARACTERS: **NARRATOR** *(behind scenes)*
CHOIR AND/OR OTHER SPECIAL SINGERS
MARY, MOTHER OF JESUS
JOSEPH
ANGEL
2 OR 3 SHEPHERDS
BOY JESUS
JOHN THE BAPTIST
PRIEST
LEVITE

MAN JESUS
2 OR 3 FOLLOWERS OF JESUS
MARY MAGDALENE
SALOME
MOB
2 SOLDIERS

COSTUMES: Biblical dress. Short white tunic with blood spots for Boy Jesus. Tattered, bloody robe for Man Jesus.

(As scene opens: Cross is stage right, hidden by screen. Stool for Mary is stage center near manger. Doll is in manger. Manger is covered by a cloth to appear as a small table. Tomb and rock are stage left. They may be concealed by low screen or plants if desired.)

CHOIR: *(Sings opening lines only of "Joy to the World")*
               Joy to the world, the Lord is come.
               Let earth receive her king.

NARRATOR: *(from Isaiah 41:16b KJV)* And thou shalt rejoice in the Lord and shalt glory in the Holy One of Israel.

PROPHET: *(enters left to center, moving trance-like with hands and face heavenward.)* Behold, a virgin shall conceive and bear a son, and shall call his name Emmanuel (Matthew 2:23 KJV). The government shall be upon his shoulders. And his name shall be called Wonderful, Counsellor, the mighty God, the everlasting Father, the Prince of Peace (Isaiah 9:6 KJV). *(exits right trance-like.)*

(MARY enters left to stool down center. Sits.)

ANGEL: *(enters right)* Hail, Mary. You are highly favored. The Lord is with you. You are blessed among women.

(MARY draws back, startled.)

ANGEL: Fear not, Mary. For you have found favor with God. You will conceive in thy womb and bring forth a son, and shall call his name Jesus. He shall be great, and shall be called the Son of the Highest God. The Lord God shall give unto him the throne of David and he shall reign over the house of Jacob for ever. Of his kingdom there shall be no end.

MARY: Let it be unto me according to thy word. *(Drops to knees, eyes closed, hands folded in prayer. Exit ANGEL.)*

CHOIR (OR MARY): *(Suggested Song: "I Am the Lord's I Know.")*

PROPHET: *(enters right, crosses trance-like behind MARY as she kneels in prayer.)* He will be despised and rejected of men; a man of sorrows and acquainted with grief. He will be wounded for our transgressions, bruised for our iniquities. With his stripes will come our healing. The Lord will lay on him the iniquity of us all, and he will be oppressed and afflicted. He will be brought as a lamb to the slaughter, but will open not his mouth. *(exits.)*

CHOIR: *(SUGGESTED SONG: a few appropriate bars of "Holy is the Lamb," or "Behold the Lamb," by Dottie Rambo)*

NARRATOR: And when the days were accomplished that she should be delivered, she brought forth her first born son, wrapped him in swaddling clothes, and laid him in a manger; because there was no room for them in the inn.

(JOSEPH enters left during narration as MARY moves to manger. JOSEPH places stool behind manger. MARY removes manger cover, sits on stool, picks up the doll, covers it gently, returns it to manger. JOSEPH kneels beside Mary.)

NARRATOR: *(as ANGEL enters down right)* In the same country where Jesus was born, shepherds were in the field watching their flocks when an angel appeared to them with this message:

ANGEL: Behold, I bring you a message of great joy for all people. Unto you is born this day in the city of David, a Saviour, which is Christ the Lord. You will find the babe wrapped in swaddling clothes, lying in a manger. All glory is given to God in the highest. He brings to earth, peace and good will. *(Exit.)*

40

(Soft MUSIC begins. Suggested SONG: "We Will Glorify.")

SHEPHERDS: *(enter right with lamb and kneel at manger.)* We praise you, Lord, for this child, and for what He means to the world. We glorify your name.

CHOIR/SINGER: *("We Will Glorify.")*

(SHEPHERDS stand, give lamb to MARY and exit.)

NARRATOR: The shepherds returned to their flocks glorifying and praising God for all they had seen and heard. They told people everywhere about the child, and about the angel who visited them with the message that this was the long-awaited savior. But Mary kept all these things and pondered them in her heart.

(MARY looks down at lamb on her lap for a few moments, then gives lamb to JOSEPH. Exit left JOSEPH with LAMB. MARY picks up "baby," and cradles him in her arms while thoughtfully "pondering" words of following VOICES.)

CHOIR: *(Suggested SONG: "Holy is the Lamb." First line softly, then continued soft background music during voices over.)*

(NOTE: The following VOICES may speak into a microphone behind scenes or be prerecorded.)

PROPHET: A virgin shall conceive and bear a son. He shall be called the son of the highest God.

ANGEL: Fear not, Mary, for you have found favor with God.

PROPHET: The Lord will lay on him the iniquities of us all.

ANGEL: Unto you is born this day, a Savior.

SHEPHERDS: We praise you, Lord, for this child. We glorify your name.

PROPHET: He will be brought as a lamb to the slaughter.

(MUSIC becomes louder. CHOIR continues "Holy is the Lamb.")

(At the close of song, MARY places "baby" in manger, spreads cloth over top of manger as before, moves slowly, thoughtfully, down right for new scene.)

BOY JESUS: *(enters left, carrying lamb)* Mother! Mother! Come quickly. He is hurt. There is blood . . .

MARY: *(head snaps up.)* Jesus! What is wrong? There is blood on your clothing. You are bleeding!

BOY JESUS: No, Mother. It is not my blood. It is the lamb's. See. Wolves attacked him. He is hurt, Mother. We must bind up his wounds.

(MARY reaches out to touch the lamb. They stand in tableau during voice of PROPHET from behind scenes or over speakers.)

PROPHET: *(Voice only)* He will be wounded for our transgressions. He will be brought as a lamb to the slaughter.

CHOIR/SINGER: *(SUGGESTED SONG: "Lamb of God," verse 1.)*

(MARY places arm around BOY JESUS, looks down at him as he soothes lamb. Exit right near end of song.)

(Enter right, JOHN BAPTIST, PRIEST, LEVITE)

PRIEST: Who are you? Are you the Christ?

JOHN: No, I am not the Christ.

PRIEST: Who then? Are you Elias the prophet returned to life?

JOHN: No, I am not Elias.

LEVITE: Then, who are you? Tell us so we may give an answer to them that sent us. Whom do you say that you are?

JOHN: I am the voice of one crying in the wilderness, Make straight the way of the Lord—just as Isaiah prophesied. The one who comes after me is preferred before me. I am not even worthy to unloose the latchet of his shoes. *(ENTER left MAN JESUS and FOLLOWERS, including MARY and other WOMEN.)*

But, look! *(Indicates Jesus with lifted hand.)* It is he of whom I speak. Behold the Lamb of God who takes away the sin of the world.

JESUS: *(earnestly to Followers as they move slowly toward center aisle to exit main sanctuary doors.)* I came down from heaven, not to do mine own will, but the will of him that sent me. Truly, I tell you, he that believeth on me hath everlasting life. I am the bread of life—the living bread which came down from heaven. If any man eat of this bread, he shall live for ever; and the bread that I will give is my flesh, which I will give for the life of the world.

In just a short while, the Son of man will be betrayed and crucified. But in three days I shall rise again. Then I shall go unto him that sent me. Although you will look for me, you will not find me. Tribulation will come. And there will come a day when the sun shall be darkened, the moon shall not give her light, the stars of heaven shall fall, and the powers that are in heaven shall be shaken. And then, shall they see the Son of man coming in the clouds with great power and glory. *(Exit.)*

CHOIR/SINGERS: *(SUGGESTED SONG: "Hallelujah, What a Savior")*

(MOB noise begins at close of song. Enter MOB through main sanctuary doors, pushing and shoving JESUS up aisle, shouting "Crucify him! Crucify him!" etc. along with taped sound. They move up aisle, still shouting, to stand offstage watching as SOLDIERS take JESUS behind the screen that conceals the cross. As SOUND of hammer begins, screen is moved to reveal JESUS on cross while SOLDIER drives nail. MARY, MARY MAGDALENE, SALOME enter left, stand watching, crying, praying.)

JESUS: Father! *(noise stops)* Father, forgive them for they know not what they are doing.

PROPHET: *(VOICE only)* He will be brought as a lamb unto the slaughter.

(Soft MUSIC begins: "Holy is the Lamb")

JESUS: Father, into thy hands I commit my spirit. *(Closes eyes, drops head.)*

(LIGHTS out, SOUND of thunder. MOB cries out in fright, moves noisily to and fro onstage to help cover movements as screen is placed to conceal cross and screen concealing tomb is removed, then EVERYONE exits noisily during darkness.)

MOB: *(might return to pews or back of sanctuary, crying out)*
What's happening?
Why has it become so dark?
It is the anger of God.
The wrath of God falls upon us.
Could it be true? Is he really the Son of God?
It must be true. We've killed the Messiah.
You are crazy. He was a mere man. A criminal. A fool.

CHOIR/SINGER: *(SUGGESTED SONG: "Were You There When They Crucified My Lord?")*

(LIGHTS on)

MARY, MARY MAGDALENE, SALOME enter right.)

MARY MAGDALENE: *(points to tomb left)* Look! The stone has been rolled away from the door.

SALOME: Why is the stone rolled away? Who could have done it?

MARY MAGDALENE: Did someone come and take away the body of our Lord?

(WOMEN look inside tomb.)

MARY MAGDALENE: He is not here. He is gone.

WOMEN: *(crying)* No! No! Our Lord is gone. They have taken him away.

JESUS: *(VOICE only)* The Son of man shall be betrayed and crucified. But in three days I will rise again. Then I shall go unto him that sent me.

MARY MAGDALENE: *(in awe)* It is true, what the Master said.

SALOME: What he told us has come to pass. He has risen.

MARY: Is he really alive?

JESUS: *(enters right.)* Mary?

MARY MAGDALENE: Master?

MARY: Jesus? Is it really you?

JESUS: Yes. It is I.

WOMEN: Master! Lord! *(fall to knees, faces to floor.)*

JESUS: Don't be afraid. Arise. Go tell my brethren to go into Galilee, and there they shall see me, too.

WOMEN: *(rise)* Yes, Lord, yes. We shall go. We will do as you say. *(Slowly back away, turn, glance back, move hurriedly toward exit.)* It is he. It is Jesus. He is alive! *(exit)*

NARRATOR: The Lamb shall overcome them, for he is Lord of Lord and King of Kings.

(MUSIC of "Holy is the Lamb" begins softly. Exit JESUS.)

NARRATOR: Worthy is the Lamb that was slain to receive power, and riches, and wisdom, and strength, and honour, and glory, and blessing.

CHOIR: *("Holy is the Lamb")*

(Invitation to worship if desired, using above scripture from Rev. 5:12. Might also use Rev. 7:17: "For the Lamb which is in the midst of the throne shall feed them, and shall lead them unto living fountains of waters: and God shall wipe away all tears from their eyes.")

45

NOTES